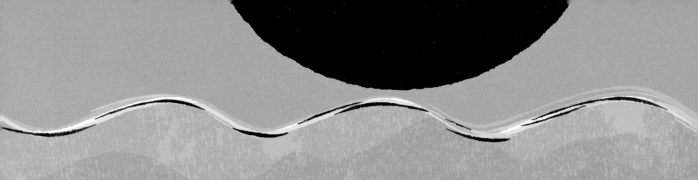

Love's wider than the ocean,

it's deeper than the sea.

Love's taller than the mountains.
It stretches way up high.

Further than the furthest star,
far beyond the sky.

Love goes on and on and on,
it fills your heart and mine.

Love's brighter than
the brightest light.

It makes the
whole world shine.

Love never, ever changes,
no matter what life brings.

Love lifts you up when you are down.
It helps you find your wings.

Love is all around you,
every single day.

And even when life gets hard,

love never goes away.

And you, my loves, have taught me
what I know to be true . . .
There is nothing bigger than
the love I feel for you.